Meet the underwater world

Welcome!!!

This book belongs to

....

Your Idea

Your Idea

Your Idea

Your Idea

Your Idea

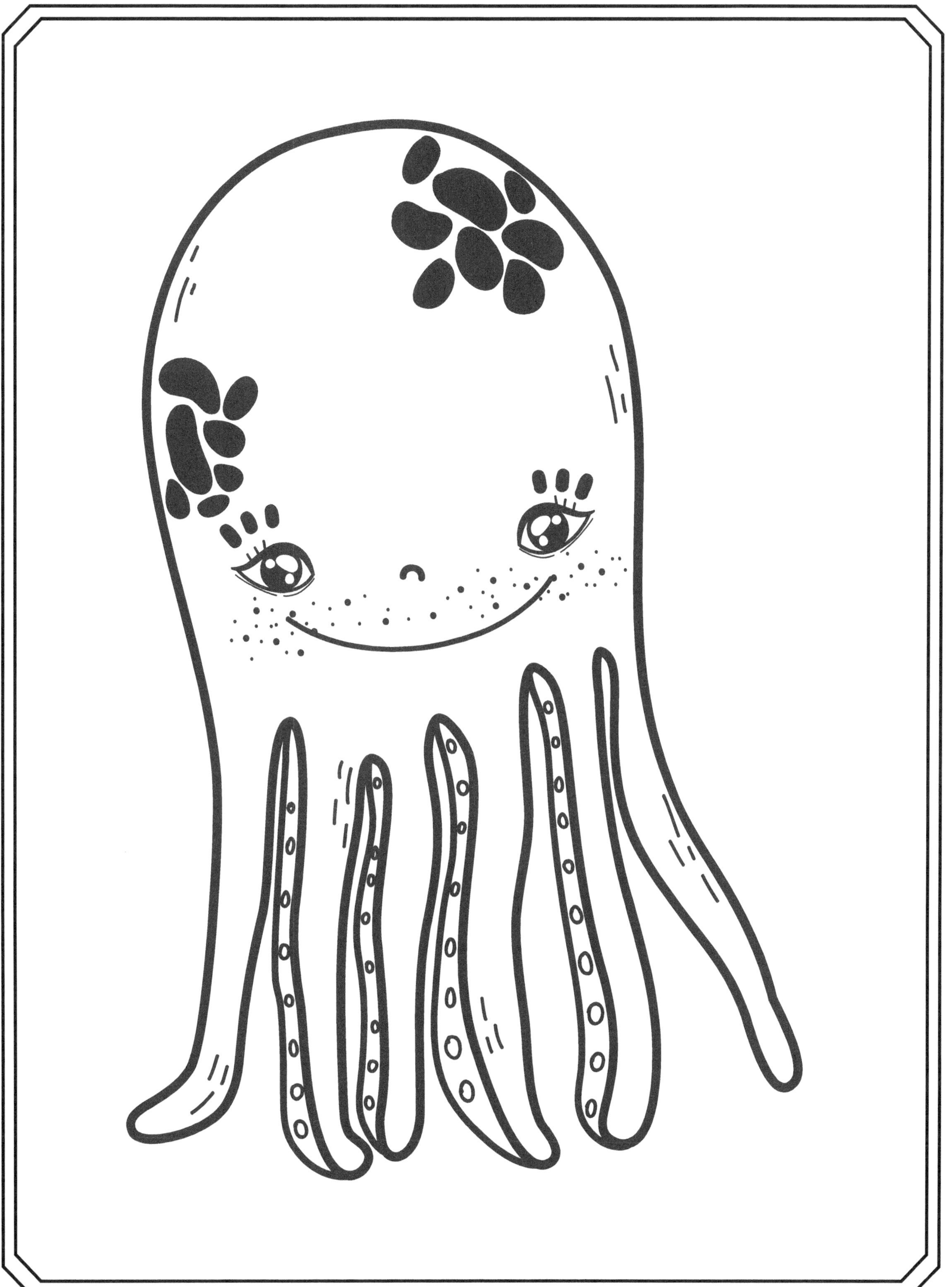

Your Idea

Your Idea

Your Idea

Your Idea

Your Idea

Your Idea

Your Idea

Your Idea

Your Idea

Your Idea

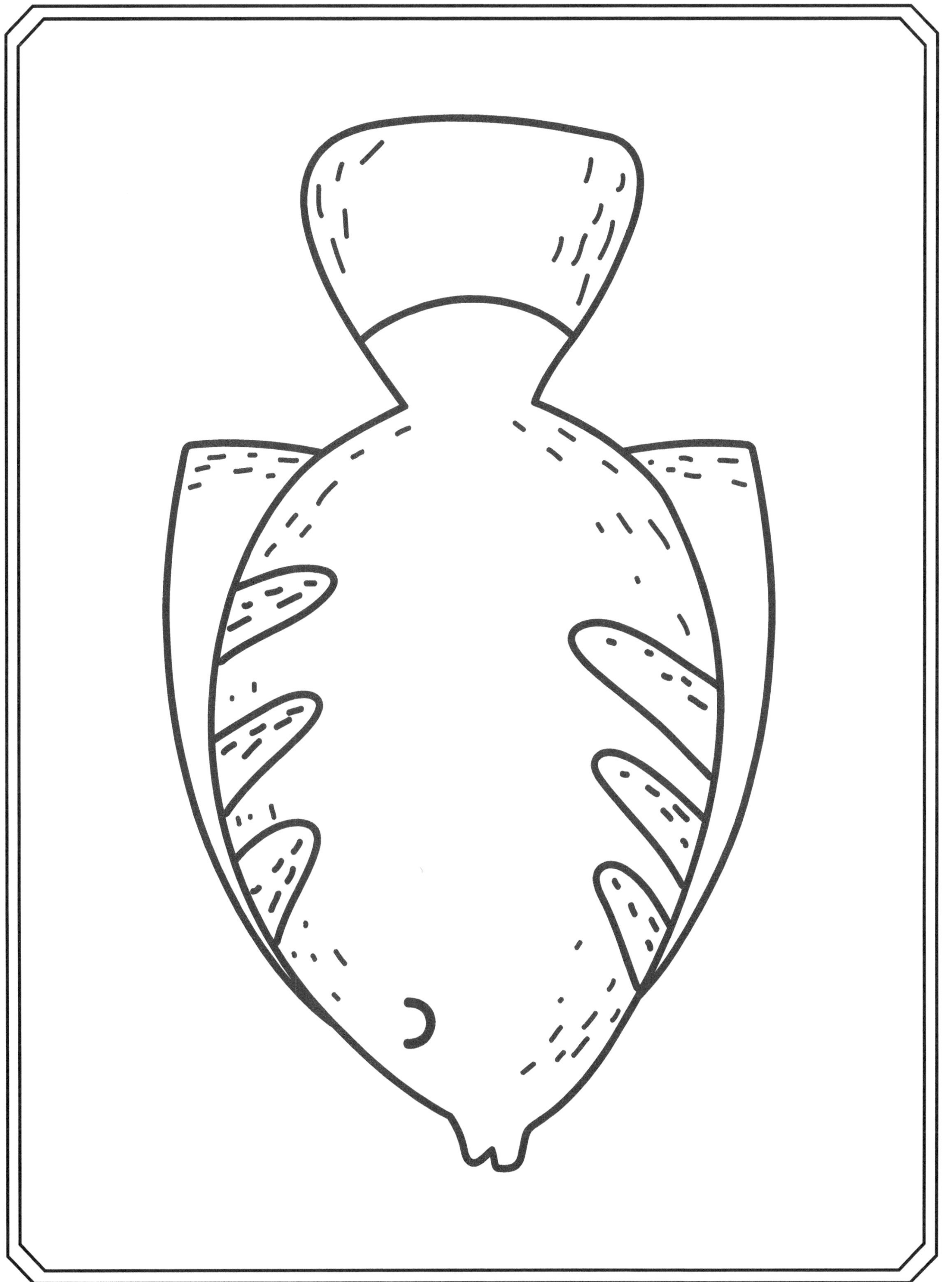

Your Idea

Your Idea

Your Idea

Your Idea

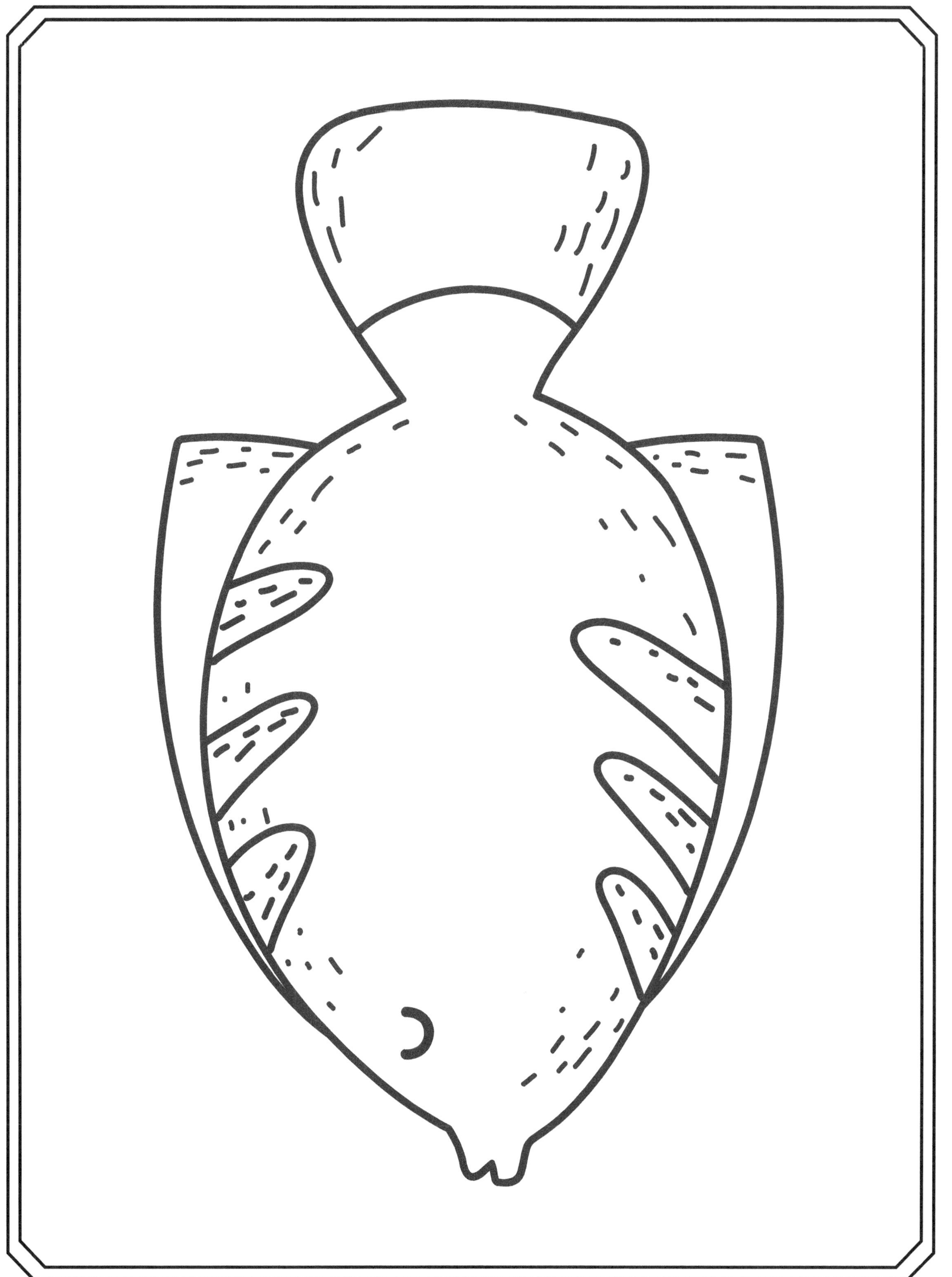

Your Idea

Your Idea

Your Idea

Your Idea

Your Idea

Your Idea

Your Idea

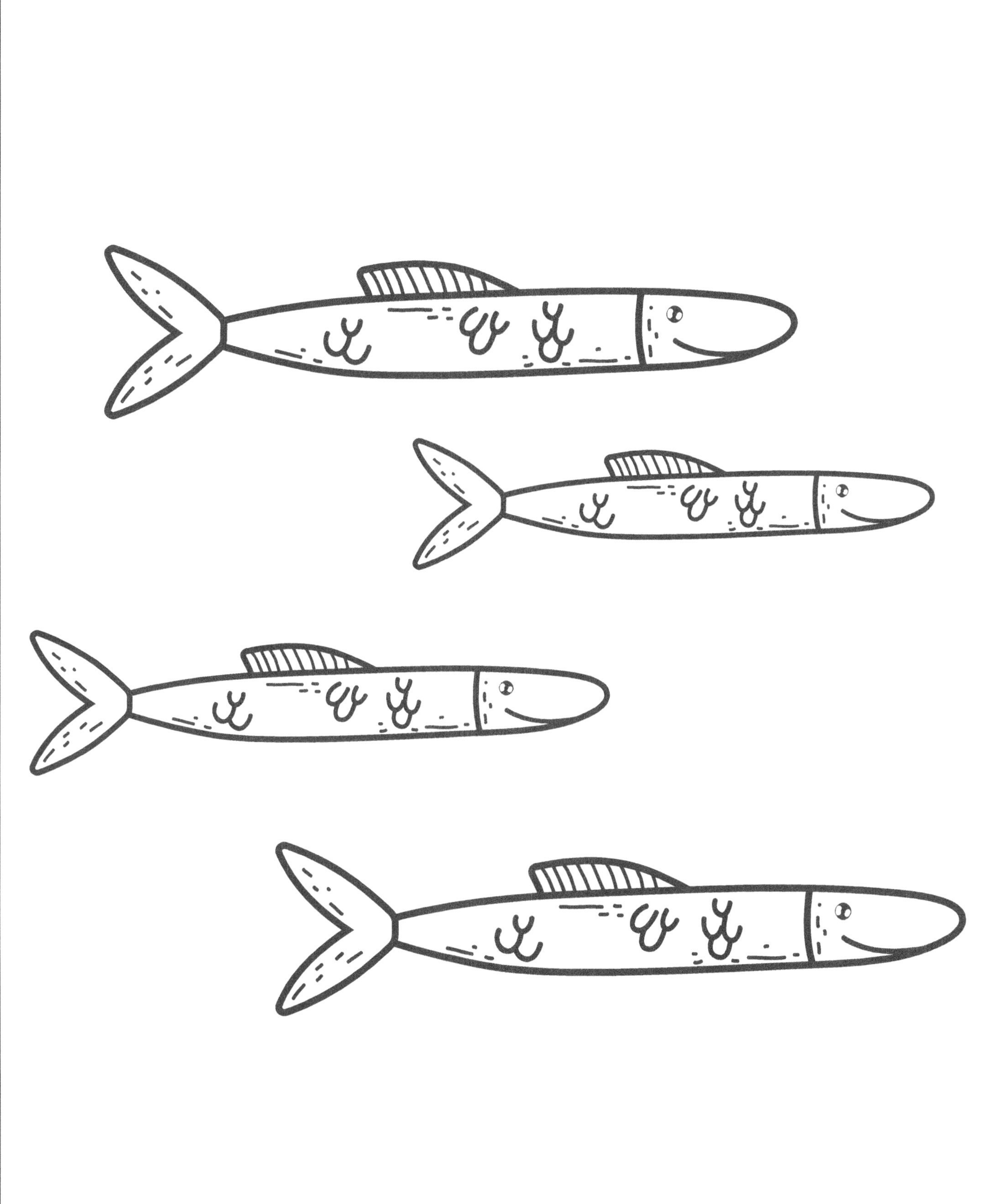

Your Idea

Your Idea

Your Idea

Your Idea

Your Idea

Your Idea

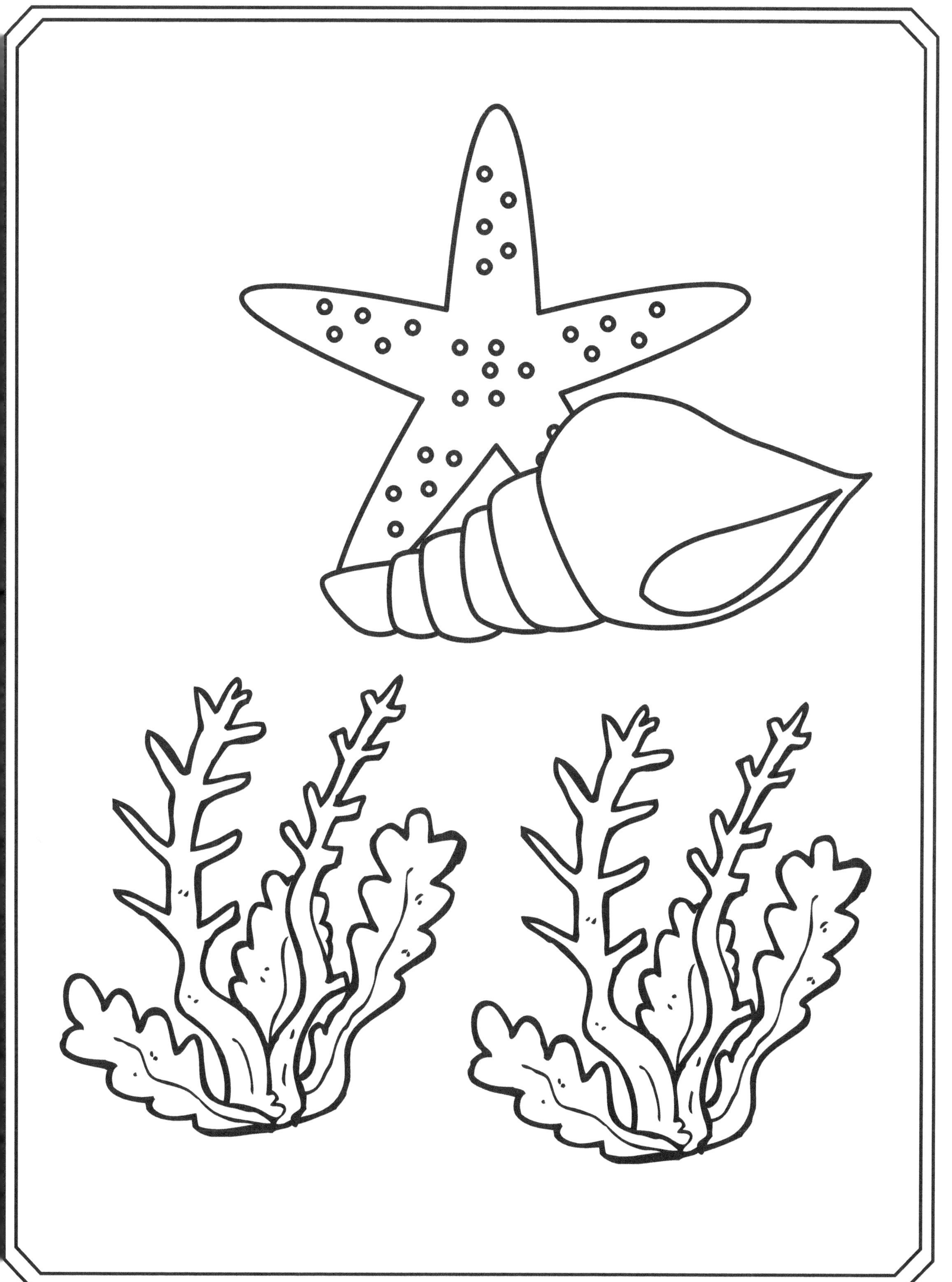

Your Idea

Your Idea

Your Idea

Your Idea

Your Idea

Your Idea

Your Idea